To Dear Dick,
(You'd never get stuck in
the shower ——— !)
From: Pat
with love

MAN IN THE SHOWER

Peter Arno

Ilse Hoffmann

PETER ARNO'S
MAN IN THE SHOWER

DUCKWORTH

This edition, with introduction by Patricia Arno Maxwell,
first published 1976 by Gerald Duckworth & Co. Ltd.
The Old Piano Factory, 43 Gloucester Crescent, London NW1
Original edition first published
by Simon and Schuster, Inc., 1944

ISBN 0 7156 1149 6

Produced by offset lithography by
UNWIN BROTHERS LIMITED
The Gresham Press, Old Woking, Surrey
A member of the Staples Printing Group

INTRODUCTION
by Patricia Arno Maxwell

The title drawing for this book was originally published in *The New Yorker* magazine on 28 August 1943, after strenuous objection and final, muttering acceptance by the editor, Harold Ross, who could not understand why the man couldn't simply open the door of the shower stall from inside, dammit, or float to the top to breathe. Arno had the pleasure and the profit of struggle with this fastidious, oblique, demanding man for many years until Ross's death in 1951, but it was Ross who gave him his start soon after the magazine began publishing in 1925.

Until then, the major influences in his life had been his gentle mother, Edith T.M. Haynes, and his father, Curtis Arnoux Peters, distinguished on the N.Y. Supreme Court bench by a case involving Eamon De Valera. Father wanted son to go into business and amount to something, not just doodle away his life as an artist. Young Arnoux, though shy and affectionate, knew what he wanted, and drew constantly. When his father divorced his mother, and remarried during the boy's last year at Hotchkiss School, the boy rebelled and estrangement was so complete that he had to leave Yale College after the first year. But he continued to draw, and the drawings fill the pages of the Hotchkiss *Mischianza* of 1921 and 1922, and the Yale *Record* and *News* of 1923. He submitted drawings to the old *Life*, to *Judge* and the *N.Y. World* without success. His strong interest in music was developing as well, and at college he formed a jazz band called the 'Yale Collegians', in which he played banjo, and Rudy Vallee began his career.

After leaving Yale, Arnoux moved to Greenwich Village, and made his living by painting murals for tearooms and nightclubs, designing sets, taking walk-on parts in plays, and even holding a 'real job', designing ads for the movie company Chadwick Pictures. He was about to accept a professional band engagement in Chicago, when he sold his first drawing for $30 to *The New Yorker* in 1925, and he knew he was on his way. He changed his name to Peter Arno, and married the glamorous writer Lois Long, who wrote reviews of nightclub life as 'Lipstick', and later created the fashion column 'On and Off the Avenue' for *The New Yorker*. They had a squalling baby girl Patricia (that's me), and a stormy time of it until their divorce in 1929. Arno married again, in 1935, and stayed with Mary 'Timmie' Lansing five years.

Between the marathon all-night, all-day sessions of drawing for *The New Yorker*, Arno managed to find time to escort some of the country's most beautiful and talented women to places like El Morocco and the Stork Club. He was immortalized in memory of some high-spirited misbehaviour, in such gossip columns as Walter Winchell's. He was voted one of the ten 'Best-Dressed Men in America' by the Custom Tailors' Guild in 1941. He designed and raced motor cars with ferocious joy, and cooked elaborate gourmet meals. He drank, and then stopped drinking entirely. He studied and visited the scenes of the Civil War and the Wild West, learning the human imperfections of such heroes as Wyatt Earp and Bat Masterson and Buffalo Bill. He wrote a musical play with E. Ray Goetz, *The New Yorkers*, in 1930, and a magnificent flop in 1931, *Here Goes The Bride*. He went through several years of psychoanalysis. He learned photography, and haunted the Ringling Bros. Barnum & Bailey Circus, for whom he illustrated their posters and souvenir programs. When World War Two interrupted the world's pleasures, and he could not serve in combat, he drew training aids and posters for the Army Air Force.

And always, through the years, there was his beloved music, which he played all night on the Steinway, composing romantic ballads that betrayed the hidden idealism he could never express otherwise. The tape machine recorded endless miles of songs by George Gershwin on piano, the orchestral music of Paul Whiteman, the songs of Helen Morgan, the banjo of Mike Pingitore from whom he learned to perfect his own banjo technique.

He painted, almost as a secret vice, and sought in slashing abstractions the austere vision of Gauguin, Rouault, and Daumier. He had some 56 one-man shows in New York, London, and Paris. But I believe he saved his most daring concepts for his drawings, and laboured over them without love, but with the savage intensity to create something impossible, his own vision of *how it should be.*

The drive to perfect his draftsmanship, the growing hatred he felt for the hypocrisy of our modern life, led him in later years to seek seclusion, and in 1951 he moved to Harrison, one hour north of the New York City that had nurtured him. There he cultivated his acre of garden with a huge tractor, his new sense of peace, his few good friends, and his grandchildren Drea and Kitty. Even when dying of cancer, he lashed out at the ministers and priests who came to 'save his soul', with his mocking humour ('I might destroy *yours*, Father!'). But his vision of how idiotic it all is, lasted until he died on 22 February 1968, and his tombstone in Valhalla, N.Y. bears a replica of his signature, 'Peter Arno', punctuating his life as it so vividly did his drawings.

April 1976   P.A.M.

"... and then I milled the slot down to thirteen-sixteenths of an inch,
exactly as the blueprint called for, and when we put the eccentric in, it fit just beautifully."

"It's all right. I'm just illustrating a point."

"She's sort of a secretary. With the new tax setup, I figure
she's only costing me eight cents on the dollar."

"Will this train take me anywhere near the Racquet Club?"

"*I'm giving you your last chance, Willis!
If your horse doesn't come in today, you're fired!*"

"Keep this under your hat —"

"It's 'Evening In Paris'."

"Dr. Carmichael! Please! Not in the Stork Club!"

"I said would you be interested in steady employment with a private family?"

"Here's to dear old Pomfret, drink 'er down, drink 'er down."

"My advice is to forget all about this and put yourself in the hands of a good tailor."

"Dammit, Parker! You might at least have said 'Ahem'!"

"You mean the Three Bears raised all that stink over a lousy bowl of breakfast food?"

"You needn't wait, Benson. I'll be some time."

"*Please step aside, sir. There's a gentleman coming out.*"

"*O'Hallihan, you know too much!*"

"Have you tried an oculist?"

"Welcome home, Colonel Bagley, suh! Welcome home!"

"*You might try our Harvard Shop.*"

"*He can't remember his name, Sergeant. All he remembers is he's somebody pretty damned important.*"

"Please, sir—this isn't my table!"

"Why, it's Mrs. Courtney Richardson, Senior—she's heading this way!"

LAUGHING HYENA

"Contagious, isn't it?"

"Refreshing bouquet, isn't it?"

"Will that be all, sir?"

"*What would I do if I were General Eisenhower? I'll tell you what I'd do if I were General Eisenhower. I'd do exactly what General Lee would have done if he'd been General Eisenhower! That's what I'd do if I were General Eisenhower, suh!*"

"*. . . just a little token of our esteem and appreciation of your six weeks of loyal service.*"

"It's been delightful having you with us, Mrs. Parkhurst."

"An' her hair was so long she could sit on it."

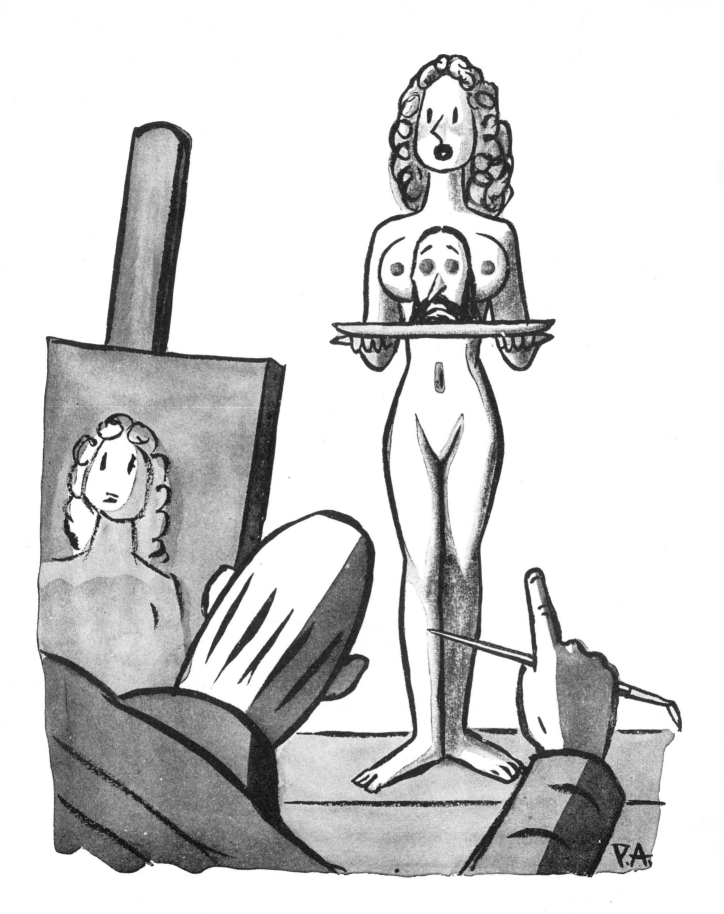

"Just a __weeeeny__ bit lower, Miss Snodgrass."

"Very good, Mr. Duncan! A month ago you couldn't have done that."

"*Young woman, do you realize my time is worth thirty dollars a minute?*"

"*Now let's get organized, Jones. Your first detail will be to set up an officers' mess.*"

"In case of an air raid, Billings, what will be done about us?"

"Oh, Mrs. Fordyce—could I trouble you to come here for a moment?"

"Thanks, no. I've had <u>more</u> than enough."

"Please! You don't understand! I'm the lifeguard!"

"Mammy's little baby loves short'nin', short'nin',
Mammy's little baby loves short'nin' bread . . ."

"*Then this is goodbye?*"

"*Well, Struthers, I guess we've gone just about as far as we can in basic English.*"

"I've received a call from St. Dunstan's-In-The-Meadow. 6500 smackers a year."

"Did you bellow, sir?"

"They're amazing!"

New Year's

"Well, I guess that breaks up our little game."

"We were fortunate in getting the after-theatre crowd, weren't we?"

"*I'm sorry, Miss, but you'll have to get off the street—until the all-clear, I mean.*"

"That reminds me of a parable they were telling in Scranton, P-A."

"Now, Arthur! No more remarks like that!"

"You can certainly tell it's her first day here!"

"Y'mean t'say there was a _file_ in that cake you sent me!"

"But where is all this leading us to, Mr. Hartman—Miami? Palm Beach? Hollywood?"

"But you're mistaken, I assure you. I was whistling for a cab."

"Now be sure and point out any celebrities."

"She seems to have a remarkable command of the language."

"Watch out for his free hand!"

"Okay, men, come out of your corners fighting. Now shake hands."

"—And do you take this able-bodied seaman for your lawful wedded husband?"

"It feels like it might be a grain of sand."

"You cad! You're not fit to touch the hem of her skirt."

"It's certainly one beautiful New Year's Day here, folks. And it's a great game these boys are playing! And is the crowd excited! Just listen to those cheers! Both teams are lining up again . . ."

"Oh dear!"

I. *The Three Musketeers*

II. *Romeo and Juliet*

III. *Macbeth*

IV. *Dr. Jekyll and Mr. Hyde*

"*I tell you we haven't got any aluminum!*"

"Why do you always get me to do the rowing, Mr. Hartley?"

"*A very good afternoon to you, sir. I represent the railroad in matters of employment.*"

"Now who shall say grace?"

"*You seem to be a clever little boy—how are you at tying knots?*"

"*No, dear, put Mamma on! Daddy hasn't time to talk to your doll baby now.*"

"Dr. Pinckney, of all people! What are you doing here?"

"Guess what happened to me an' the truck, boss! . . . No. . . .
No. . . . No, guess again."

"Beg pardon, sir, but have you noticed Mr. Hopkins seems to be settling slowly to the right?"

"These yours?"

"*Frisbee said I could go ahead and let him have the old one-two if it would give me any pleasure.*"

"When do the celebrities start fighting?"

"*Mrs. Choate's just fine, thank you. How's Mrs. Delano?*"

"*Say, that's funny, gentlemen. The same danged thing happened to my daughter Emmy!*"

"*I want to report a tornado.*"

"If a woman shows up looking for a little boy who's lost,
I'll be in the toy department."

"This seems like a good place."

"Oh come now—a little Pousse Café never hurt anyone!"

"Just what do they mean by 'untouchable'?"

"You and your rapier-like wit!"

"They produce a fascinating rhythm, don't they?"

"Pardon me. Have you seen any condor eggs?"

"Be careful. The place is simply lousy with mistletoe!"

"*She's a very famous starlet. I hear they're even considering putting her in a picture.*"

"*Visiting hours are over, Mr. Kugelman.*"

"I don't see how the farmer's daughter ever had time to meet <u>anybody</u>!"

"*May we be excused for a few minutes, Mamma? I want to show Miss deWalden the new septic tank.*"

"*Mercy, the doctor certainly keeps you on the go, doesn't he?*"

"*I tell you we're on our way to Estes Park! We had no idea we were parked near an Army camp.*"

"Don't you just <u>adore</u> it?"

" . . . so frankly, Mr. Baumgarten, I won't be needing your help from now on."

"Hold on there! I answer the questions around here."

"*Is that one?*"

"He's too damn calm and collected to suit _me_. _I_ think we're lost."

"*Did anyone ever tell you, Miss Kapmann, that your eyes are the color of our best grade off-blue No. 3 yarn?*"

"*What you need is more fresh air and exercise. How would you like to caddie for me this weekend?*"

"My goodness! Your dear old uncle seems to have left everything to me."

THE END